I0503569

PASSIVE INCOME SECRETS

Make Money While You Sleep

Justin Harrison

FOREWORD

I t's no secret that Passive Income is the one thing that all of us are after. It's the one thing that will allow you to live life on your own terms and not having to trade your time for money.

Unlike most programs about passive income, Justin gives you the solid truth. He is open and honest with you and explains why passive income is the closest thing to free money but in the same breath, that it does in fact take hard work initially to get there.

It can be overwhelming when we start looking into passive income because of the mass amount of information out there but Justin manages to make you look at this differently.

By explaining the different kinds of passive income types and giving you real-life examples, he guides you towards deciding which option is best for you. Apart from this, he gives you 100 awesome passive income ideas that you can start right now.

At the end of the book, he gives you an eye-opening reality check and a solid kick up the butt by encouraging you to get your side hustle on.

I have known Justin for well over 10 years and I know he is living proof of this. Justin lives life on his own terms, travels when and where he wants and doesn't have to trade his time for money. He practices what he preaches.

This is by far the best guide I have read about passive income and the advice that you get from this book could be life-changing if you follow his advice.

David Bester

TABLE OF CONTENTS

INTRODUCTION

One of the easiest ways to gain your financial independence is to reconfigure your life so that a substantial portion of your income is not actively earned by your labour and time.

Additionally, passive income is attractive because it frees up your time so you can focus on the things you actually enjoy.

In a nutshell, passive income is money received that requires little or no effort to maintain the flow of income once the initial work has been done.

If people in most professions want to earn the same amount of money and enjoy the same lifestyle year after year, they must continue to work the same number of hours at the same pay rate, or more, to keep up with inflation.

Once you decide to retire or find yourself unable to work any longer, your income will stop, unless you have some form of passive income. In the old days, this was easily accomplished with participation in company-sponsored pension plans, but those are far less common today, and mostly unreliable.

Most people find it extremely difficult to build up a reliable source of passive income, and it has been my personal experience when coaching people that a lot of this has to do with people's personal perception that making money is "hard" and that making money should involve lots of effort.

Passive income by its very nature is easy money. Sure it requires some effort and time or money invested initially, but thereafter if you do things right, the money should come no matter how much or how little effort you put in.

For most people, this is a foreign concept, even if that's what they deeply desire, society has brainwashed us into believing that we need to constantly exchange "sweat equity" in order to earn money.

The thing is that people earning passive income often feel guilty when they earn money for doing nothing other than the initial setup. Easy money goes against the grain of this work hard culture that we have.

Maybe your parents worked really hard for their money, maybe it feels weird to make money easy, or maybe you feel guilty that other people in your world don't have the same opportunities and vision as you.

Now, this is the critical part, the part that will either turn you into a passive income master or send you back into the sweat equity trenches.

The most important thing for you to work on right now is your mental block around earning easy money, earning money for doing nothing.

I am by no means suggesting it's going to be easy, and I am by no means suggesting it requires zero effort. What I am saying is that you have to learn to deal with the idea that once you set something up that you will earn for doing very little, and that should neither make you feel guilty nor complacent.

Passive income is an awesome thing, it's changed my life for the better in every conceivable way. I stopped worrying about money, I stopped worrying about income security.

I've been able to travel the world with my family, make money even when I'm not working, or when I wanted to start a family or take a break from working altogether.

In this book, I am going to hold you by the hand and guide you towards your ideal passive income, and I promise you this, passive income will change your life, if you're willing to change your mindset around it, and it will give you the most incredible sense of freedom you will ever know.

Let's get started.

WHAT IS PASSIVE INCOME

P assive income is highly sought after and often misunderstood. Passive income isn't free money, but rather a steady stream of income that requires little to no effort on your part, once you have done the "initial setup".

Passive income streams require an upfront investment and a lot of nurturing in the beginning. After some time and hard work, these income streams start to build and are able to maintain themselves, bringing you consistent revenue without much effort on your part.

Although the word "passive" makes it sound like you have to do nothing to bring in the income, this just isn't true. All passive income streams will require at least one of the following two elements:

- An upfront monetary investment, or
- An upfront time investment

You simply won't be able to produce and earn residual passive income without being willing to invest at least one of these two initial elements, however, when done correctly these upfront investments will produce passive income for years to come with very little ongoing effort required.

This brings us to the next point. There is a misconception that passive income requires absolutely no ongoing effort, and that is also simply not true.

Passive income needs to be managed, but unlike traditional income, you are not directly trading your time for income, which means you can have several passive incomes and leverage your time accordingly.

WHY STRIVE FOR PASSIVE INCOME

Money buys happiness. Not because of the things it can buy. In fact, it's likely the more money you have, the more you realize you can't buy anything material that will provide you with sustained happiness.

Rather, money buys the freedom to pursue your dreams. Money empowers your ability to jump out of bed each morning to choose exactly how you're going to add value to the world.

One of life's biggest traps is that we're programmed to only exchange our time and effort for money. We're set up to believe this is the end goal for our lives and for our careers.

This starts at an early age when we're asked: "What are you going to be when you grow up?" This question implies: "How do you want to exchange time and effort for money when you grow up?"

The irony is: we trade so much of our time and effort for money, the only thing we're taught to do with money is to spend it.

We all have to work to make money at some point in our lives. However, most people think of this as the endpoint and not a stage in their lives when they should be accumulating assets that create passive income as quickly as possible, so they can buy their freedom. That is, freedom to exchange time and effort to pursue their passions.

We can get out of this trap if we learn to build passive income streams when we are young. This can set us free to spend our time and effort to add value by pursuing our passions.

If you can generate enough passive income to pay for all the things you need to make you happy, then you are rich. That is, you have complete freedom to choose how you add value to the world each day!

Passive income means freedom, and you owe it to yourself and your family to prioritize and make sure you have several sources of passive income. When you do, you will have the time to spend on what you really want to do in life.

The additional benefit of having passive income is that you will never be stressed about money, and there will be even more opportunities that come your way.

When you have money constantly flowing your way, you will make it your business to activate the money again and again and again.

Of course, you should automate your savings and investments so that they happen automatically for you, then once your savings and investments are growing, you can become more creative about how to make your money work for you, and how to add additional streams of income.

But one thing that's guaranteed, the more passive income you have, the more ideas of making additional passive income you will come across.

Most people spend their entire lives working, trading time and labour for money, only to retire, tired, old and having missed out on having lived an amazing life for no other reason than that they were limited by having to trade their time for money.

Ask around in an old age home, or ask people on their deathbeds, and I assure you not one person will suggest they regret not having worked more.

The true secret to happiness is finding a way to create secure sources of passive income that allows you to live without stress and to pursue your passion without having to worry about paying bills.

Passive income truly is a ticket to freedom.

PASSIVE INCOME STRATEGIES

T here are three key strategies for generating passive income. Some people choose to use a combination of these or only one depending on their individual situations, these strategies are:

PASSIVE INCOME BY INVESTMENT:

As the name suggests, this form of passive income generation involves taking the money you already have and investing it to produce a passive income, essentially this is known as "putting your money to work".

Typically this route towards passive income generation is taken by people who have either inherited money, taken a severance package at work or received some other large lump sum payout.

Other people who also consider this option are highly paid professionals such as doctors, lawyers, accountants, pilots etc.

The basic idea here is that their time is more valuable than money, and they have the money to invest instead of their time, and therefore use the money they have available as a vehicle to generate passive income.

PASSIVE INCOME BY CREATIVITY:

This form of passive income generation is typically focused more on the artistic and literary pursuits. Although that its a rather limiting explanation of the broader category, examples include authors, music producers, composers, artists, voice-over artists and anyone who gets paid ongoing royalties for creative work they created once off.

Typically this route is followed more by people driven by their passions rather than people driven by the pursuit of passive income, however many people have pursued a creative passion a secondary career that has ultimately resulted in a strong passive income.

Passive income through creative pursuits can not only be extremely financially rewarding, but they can offer a sense of self-achievement that cannot be gained merely by investing money to achieve passive income.

PASSIVE INCOME BY EFFORT IDEAS:

As the name suggests, this form of passive income is built based on you trading your time and effort rather than your money or creativity in order to build a passive income stream. Examples of this include, time exchanged for equity in a business or labour invested in a startup in exchange for shares.

Typically this route is followed by people who find themselves working for a company during the early-stage development of the business and who share a common vision with the founders and forgo some or all of their salaries in exchange for equity in the long term.

Other examples include people who consult for companies and do not require compensation in the form of money but rather in the form of equity.

GET YOUR SIDE HUSTLE ON

One of the best things about developing a passive income is that it should not require your constant attention, which means that you can develop an additional revenue stream while doing your ordinary work and taking care of normal business which brings your primary income.

Getting your side hustle on is about strategically using your time, and ensuring you invest (be it time or money) into endeavours that will yield a maximum return for minimal long term effort.

The next time you ask someone what they do for a living, you might want to follow it up with a second question, and ask what their side hustle is. These days, many people have one, and you will likely be surprised at the answers.

A good friend of mine who is a senior sales executive of a national company spends his weekends taking off-road vehicle tours and doing advanced driver training, while another friend spends his off-hours buying and flipping sports memorabilia and other collectables on the side.

Building a successful side gig isn't always easy. With a little time and some helpful hints from the folks who've done it before, you can launch a passion project that turns into a steady passive income that not only supplements your income but provides you with additional income to further invest and create the financial freedom you have always dreamed of having.

As with most things in life, time management is going to be your biggest challenge, and you will most likely have to prioritize your side hustle initially over other things you enjoy during your normal downtime.

However, I assure you, the time invested initially into your side hustle will pay for itself later down the line when you gain the freedom to do what you want on your terms.

PASSIVE INCOME BY INVESTMENT IDEAS

1. Invest in Real Estate:

Real estate can be a great way to make money while you sleep. However, I decided to buy a couple of rental properties in my early twenties and I had a much different experience. I had a bad tenant who was late on his rent all the time, constant plumbing problems, and I even had to evict a tenant. It was not as amazing as I thought it would be.

Since then I have gravitated more towards group property investment schemes such as property funds, crowdfunding real estate ventures, and private property equity funds.

Some examples are Fundrise, which allows you to invest from $500 upwards in more than 48 real estate products through a real estate investment trust, and AcreTrader which will let you invest in farmland with as little as $5,000

Many of these group investments have between an 8%- 9% return, they also have a gross cash yield between 3-4%.

2. Dividend Income:

Dividend income is money paid to shareholders of stocks in the form of cash. Dividend-paying stocks are especially enticing for those wanting to make a living with passive income, as they will get pay-outs each quarter or so. Even Warren Buffet historically is a fan of dividend-paying stocks.

If you are going to go this route, make sure that you educate yourself and pick solid stocks so that you can depend on for dividend income for years to come.

If you don't have an investment account check out **eTorro**, you can invest in single stocks and mutual funds with zero brokers fees.

3. Peer-to-Peer Lending:

Peer-to-peer lending is when you loan people money directly through an online platform which manages the loan and ensures you get paid.

There are several excellent peer-to-peer lending platforms including LendingClub, Peerform, Worthy. Etc. Do a Google search for peer-to-peer lending platforms and you are sure to find plenty of options.

4. Open a High-Yield Account:

Are you looking for a low-risk way to make income passively? Then look at opening a high-yield savings account with a bank outside of your country in a developing country with a stable economy such as Georgia, Lithuania etc.

5. Invest In Vending Machines:

A successful vending machine business can be a great way to make passive income. The key is to find the right places to install your vending machines. Check with smaller brick and mortar businesses. Contact those that have over 100 workers in the building on a daily basis, and see if they need vending machines. Another key to vending machine success, ask those workers what items they prefer to have in the vending machine and then stock accordingly. Once again, if you want to reduce the amount of time that you are involved, consider hiring someone to stock the machines for you.

6. Buy an Established Online Business:

The beauty of an online business is that most will allow you to work from anywhere. Starting one from scratch can take a lot of time and resources. Why not consider buying an already established online business? Websites such as Biz Buy Sell have hundreds of online business listings that are for sale in varying price ranges.

Check to see if there is an online business for sale that is in line with your passions or hobbies. Again, in order for this idea to produce passive income, you'll need to hire someone to run the business.

7. Rent Your Stuff Out:

Thousands of people every day are looking to rent any variety of items, and simply creating some classifieds listings can bring a lot of business for you.

Here are some product ideas that you could rent out: extension ladders, party tents, tables and chairs, utility trailers, chainsaws etc. You can even rent out your car when you are not using it with a company like Turo.

Just make sure that you have a proper rental agreement signed by both parties. Also, get paid in cash beforehand, and get a current photo ID and secondary proof of address from renters.

This will help you to protect the property you're renting out. For extra peace of mind, consider requesting a security deposit as well.

8. Self Service Car Wash:

A self-service car wash is a basic car wash that is basic cinder blocks, a pressure washer and is coin-operated. If you're going to run a proper car wash with staff it's definitely a business vs. a passive income stream and not the same thing as a self-service car wash.

9. Self Storage Unit Rentals:

You can either invest directly into building or buying storage units or If you're not sure about getting into this space, you can also invest in storage rentals via a REIT. FundRise invests in commercial properties like storage rentals and you can get started for as little as $500.

10. Become A Silent Investor / Partner:

There are so many horror stories of people investing in their mate's pub, restaurant or whatever that the idea totally freaks most people out. However, if done correctly with the right partners, and managed well this can be one of the most lucrative passive investments you can make.

The key to success here is finding the right people to invest in, doing your due diligence and making sure you constantly keep tabs on the financial situation within the business to make sure your investment is well managed.

11. Crowdfunded Farming:

Crowdfunded farming works the same as crowdfunded real estate. Essentially you help farmers by investing in their farms, crops and livestock for a share of the profits, which can be extremely lucrative. Examples of places where you can invest include CropCapital and LivestockWealth.

12. Invest In Airport Parking Spaces:

Investing in airport car parking is a safe way to invest your money, and it produces a higher ROI than traditional investment strategies. Up to 17%, in some cases, and airport parking is estimated to be worth $12.5 billion annually, with demand regularly outstripping supply. Additionally, parking spaces have huge projected capital growth, thanks to market demand.

13. Start & AirBnB Sideline Business:

This could be as simple as transforming an outside room in your house into a room that you rent out on Airbnb, or buying and transforming properties into fully managed AirBnB properties. There are literally an endless amount of opportunities for unique, well priced and creative spaces on Airbnb.

14. Start Mining Cryptocurrency Coins:

Cloud mining offers a mechanism to mine a cryptocurrency such as bitcoin without having to install all the hardware and related paraphernalia. There are companies that allow people to open an account with them and participate in the process of cloud mining for a basic cost. The process makes mining accessible to a wider number of people across distant locations and provides an opportunity for anyone to earn crypto income from mining.

PASSIVE INCOME BY CREATIVITY IDEAS

1. Sell An eBook Online:

When you purchase an eBook off of Amazon there's a pretty good chance you're buying a self-published book. Self-publishing is actually very easy. To self-publish a book you'll first need to write and edit it, create a cover, and then upload to a program such as Amazon's Kindle Direct Publishing. Don't expect instant success though.

There will need to be a lot of upfront marketing before you can turn this into a passive income stream, but with the right effort and marketing, you could create an excellent passive income stream.

2. Create A Course On Udemy:

Udemy is an online platform that lets its users take video courses on a wide array of subjects. Instead of being a consumer on Udemy you can instead be a producer, create your own video course, and allow users to purchase it. This is a fantastic option if you are highly knowledgeable in a specific subject matter. This can also be a great way to turn traditional tutoring into a passive income stream that is completely automated.

3. Selling Stock Photos:

Do you ever wonder where websites, blogs, and sometimes even magazines get their photos? These are normally bought from stock photo websites. If you enjoy photography you can submit your photos to stock photo sites and receive a revenue share every time someone purchases one of your photos.

4. Licensing Music:

Just like stock photos you can license and earn a royalty off your music when someone chooses to use it. People can either purchase your music via a license to use in their projects, or they can agree to share advertising revenue with you on platforms like YouTube in exchange for using your music.

5. Create A Mobile App:

Have you ever had an amazing idea for a mobile app? If so, you could consider hiring a programmer to create your app for you. Once your app is created, you can then get it listed in the app stores and start selling it.

6. Design And Sell T-Shirts:

Sites like CafePress allow users to custom design items like T-shirts. If your design becomes popular and makes sales you'll be able to earn royalties.

Even Amazon has a new service called Amazon Merch, where you simply upload your designs and Amazon takes care of the rest (making it, packing it, and shipping it), which means your income is truly passive.

7. Sell Digital Files On Etsy:

You can sell virtually any digital file you have created and own on Etsy. Examples include wall art, excel templates, word templates, graphic file templates, and more. The list is endless and can provide an excellent source of passive income if you supply what people are looking for.

8. Create A Blog:

Find a subject you are passionate and knowledgeable about, start a blog and get writing. Attract an audience and then start adding some advertising and affiliate links to produce passive income.

9. Start A YouTube Channel:

Much like creating a blog, find a subject you are passionate and knowledgeable about and start making videos on the subject. Attract an audience and then start adding some advertising and affiliate links to produce passive income.

10. Turn Your Car Into An Advert:

Here is a fantastic idea to help you get paid for doing something you already do every single day, driving your car. You can get paid to display advertisers branding on your car, and there are even dedicated market paces like Carvertise and Wrapify that will connect you with potential advertisers.

11. Become A Brand Ambassador:

If you are passionate about something, maybe a sport, cooking, a computer game and you think you have what it takes to represent a brand you are extremely fond of, why not approach them for free products, and possibly getting a paid gig as a brand ambassador and get paid to do what you already love doing and talking about anyway.

12. Become A Social Media Influencer:

Social media has become a big business and brands are investing in people who have reach and influence. So why not build a profile for yourself in a niche that you are passionate about. Love fly fishing, why not build a youtube channel, Instagram account, or Facebook page around the subject and create a brand around yourself so that you can get paid as a social media influencer to talk about stuff that you already love and do every day.

13. Create & Sell Ringtones:

People love ringtones, in fact, annually $1.9 billion is spent on ringtone purchases alone. So why not get creative, come up with some of your own ringtones and put these in the marketplace. You will be surprised at what people will purchase to be different. Remember the Heineken "what's uuuup" tagline, or the farting cat, those ringtones sold by the millions.

14. Turn Your Photos into Canvas Art:

Canvass art is a big business and if you love taking photos you can take those unique pictures and turn them into canvas prints and sell them online. Sites like Pictorem and Pixoto allow you to create your own canvas shop with little to no risk because you only print when someone orders.

PASSIVE INCOME BY EFFORT IDEAS

1. Consult in Exchange for Equity:

If you have a particular strength or skill that you already use, maybe in your own business or in the course of your current employment, you could put that skill to work after hours working for other companies.

However, instead of getting paid cash in exchange for your services rendered you could negotiate an equity exchange either based on the number of hours provided, or on the result you bring to the business. This is particularly attractive to companies that are looking to attract the best talent.

It does not matter if you are in finance, marketing, logistics, hr, or any other form of operations you can leverage your time for equity, and since you won't be getting paid, you can have an open relationship with the company you are providing your services to.

2. Coach in Exchange for Equity:

Much like the consulting for equity idea, this involves working with teams or individuals. Examples include business leaders, singers, actors, artists and other talented individuals.

If you believe that someone has what it takes to succeed under your guidance consider negotiating an upfront contract where you provide your services to them now in exchange for equity in future earnings, essentially like royalties.

3. Become A Local Business Marketer:

Most local businesses do not have the resources or the knowledge to keep up with modern-day marketing, specifically digital marketing. Consider finding business in your local area where you can provide social media and digital marketing services in exchange for equity or a share of the profits.

Not only will this reduce their risk and make them less reluctant to invest in marketing, but this will create a massive opportunity for you to have a stake in multiple businesses with very little risk.

4. Setup A Lead Generation Business:

Consider creating a lead generation business for local services in your area where you get paid for every enquiry you send to the local businesses. You can create a website, a directory, even an app that connects people with the services they need, from a plumber to an electrician.

These lead generation businesses take a bit of work to set up, but once they are running they continue to produce returns for years to come because they provide an invaluable service connecting consumers with the exact services providers they are needing, at the exact time they need them.

45 ADDITIONAL PASSIVE INCOME IDEAS

- Royalties from audiobooks
- Royalties from print on demand paperback books
- Royalties from article writing
- Royalties from audio samples
- Royalties from songwriting
- Royalties from soundtracks
- Advertising on freemium apps
- Sales from subscription-based audio content
- Sales from audio content
- Sales from selling membership only content
- Capital gains from collectables
- Rental income from P2P car lending
- Profits from a dropshipping store
- Profits from a POD store
- Profits from a POD market place store
- Profits from a coin-operated laundromat
- Profits from coin-operated game machines
- Profits from retail arbitrage
- Profits from Airbnb arbitrage

- Profits from service arbitrage
- License and royalty fees from a franchise
- License fees from SAAS
- Cashback from shopping apps
- Rewards from loyalty programs on spending
- Reward programs for air miles
- Sell advertising space on property
- Sell excess electric from solar power
- Buy a profitable Kindle Direct Publishing account
- Buy a profitable Createspace account
- Buy a profitable ACX (Audio Publishers) account
- Buy a profitable Amazon seller account
- Buy the rights of profitable intellectual property
- Commissions from MLM sales
- Commissions from a broker website
- Run a trailer park
- Run a cyber cafe
- Run coin-operated arcade games
- Run a solar farm
- Run a no-frills 24/7 fitness centre
- Transaction fees from hosting an ATM machine

- Transaction fees from a marketplace site
- Donations for niche related content
- Automate an active business model
- Management fees from a savings club
- Get paid to share your CPU capacity online

CLOSING THOUGHTS

There are only two ways to become financially independent or as some people call it "rich", either you make a lot of money fast, or you find a way to create passive income to live the lifestyle you have always wanted. **It really is as simple as that!**

The conventional wisdom goes like this: Keep a budget, save 10% of your income, don't spend on any extravagances (especially not coffee, the most evil of all), invest your money, don't use credit cards, and buy a house because it's a "good investment." and somehow, someday, you'll be financially secure. Not rich, just okay!

Never mind that very few fucking people have the discipline to save 10% of their income. Never mind that each of those recommendations depends on sheer fucking willpower, which let's face it unless you're a monk, it will only last for a month or two before it dissipates as predictably as the effects of diets.

Most of us know behavioural change is extraordinarily challenging and few people study how it actually works. Yet "financial experts" continue spouting off this bullshit of saving and trying harder through sheer force alone. Why?

Because it's easy to write, requires very little energy to consume from a largely apathetic and semi–financially-conscious public. Real behavioural change takes systems, not simply willpower. Real behavioural change requires conscious spending, not across-the-board cost-cutting.

The ordinary wisdom of "stop wasting your money on stuff" is filled with outdated cliches like encouraging us to stop spending on coffee, eating out, and all the things that people spend money on as a natural part of life.

Even more importantly, we're all embedded in a social system that reinforces this spending, making it virtually impossible to cut down discretionary expenses by willpower alone. This is like telling teens to stop having sex: You can try, and it may make you feel better to say it, but that's not going to change the actual numbers (with the exception of my kids of course).

In fact, if I had followed the expert's advice alone, stopped eating out, cooked at home every day, never gone on vacation, used 1 ply toilet paper instead of 2 ply, walked everywhere, and re-used everything including my teabags, I may have more money in the bank, but I would be one miserable son of a bitch who never lived, who never explored and who never truly loved life.

So here is the fucking downright dirty truth nobody is telling you. Your life is shit because you don't earn enough money. Your life has stress because you don't earn enough money. You don't save enough, because you don't have enough disposable income.

So quit fucking about brothers and sisters, quit sitting on the couch with your finger up your ass on a Saturday afternoon complaining, get a spark up your arse and get your goddam side hustle on.

ACKNOWLEDGEMENTS

I would like to thank my business partners, Dale Maxwell, Laura Palmeri, David Bester and Chris du Toit who have held down the fort while I took the time to write this book. Without their support and input, this book would never have become a reality.

I would especially like to thank Laura for her critical eye and constant proofreading, which helps a dyslexic, barely literate guy like myself seem capable of writing something worth reading.

I would also like to extend an extra-special thank you to my wife Andrea who as always offers constant constructive criticism and input, and unwavering support. Thank you for always making sure I have no distractions when I write and for your total commitment. I could not have asked for a better partner.

Last but not least, I would like to give an extra heartfelt thank you to David for sharing my vision and helping bring these ideas to life. Your work

ethic and dedication to Global Money Academy is
inspiring.

First printing, 2019.
Team 6 Investment Holdings Ltd.
5th Floor, Ritter House,
Wickhams Clay II,
Road Town, Tortola
British Virgin Islands

www.globalmoneyacademy.com